WALKING ON WATER

WALKING ON WATER

Britney Samuel

Copyright © 2024 Britney Samuel

All rights reserved

No part of this book may be reproduced, or stored in a retrieval system, or transmitted in any form or by any means, electronic, mechanical, photocopying, recording, or otherwise, without express written permission of the publisher.

Scripture quotations taken from The Holy Bible, New International Version®
NIV®
Copyright © 1973, 1978, 1984, 2011 by Biblica, Inc.
Used with permission. All rights reserved worldwide.

Scripture taken from the New King James Version®. Copyright © 1982 by Thomas Nelson. Used by permission. All rights reserved.

ISBN-13: 9798332012075

Library of Congress Control Number: 2018675309
Printed in the United States of America

CONTENTS

Walking On Water	
Title Page	
Copyright	
Foreword	
A letter to my Daddy.	1
Them or Me?	3
Self-discovery:	9
Passing of the torch.	15
The Betrayal….	20
The birth of Trust, Obey & Imagine Ministries.	24
Walking on Water.	34
Sometimes you have to lose, to win again !	42
12 Month Preparation:	47
Epilogue: God did it!	49

FOREWORD

Britney Samuel was born on February 8,1988 and raised in Newark Delaware for the majority of her life. She is the middle child and the only girl of two other siblings. She was raised by both of her parents. She graduated from Newark high school in the year of 2007. She worked several jobs throughout her life before becoming a full time entrepreneur working for the Lord .

She is a divorced single mother of 3 beautiful children London is(from previous relationship), Britain and Emmanuel are from ex-husband. She wore the title of "Miss. independent woman " very well until one day she made a decision to answer the call from the Lord over her life and became FULLY dependent and reliant upon the Lord. She's always been known for her crazy faith, her super bubbly personality and her optimistic outlook on life .

She has been such a huge inspiration to many people and has a passion to spread love , kindness and the gospel of Jesus Christ to the world.

A LETTER TO MY DADDY.

Dear Daddy,
I want you to know that I miss you so much and I love you so much. I know we didn't really get a chance to say our nal goodbyes to eachother and I'm okay with that because I know that goodbye means forever. And I know one day soon I will see you again. There's not a day that goes by that I don't think of you. Sometimes it's still feels unreal that you're no longer on this earthly realm. You passed me the torch, and it is my duty to carry on your legacy and break every single barrier that you may have been afraid to break. I want you to know that despite not having the family that I grew up with, that I'm doing just ne and God has blessed me with a wonderful family who truly supports, honors and appreciates me. This book is in honor and dedication to you. Everything that I'm doing is not only for obedience to the Lord but it is also to make you proud and to break off the generational curses off of our bloodline and the generations to come. Thank you for doing the best you could do as a father. You planted the seed in me and it has grown and now I am thriving and flourishing in the Lord. Rest peacefully daddy, we shall meet again. Thank you for being the best dad you could be to me and teaching me the way of the Lord. I love you so much.

Love,

Kooty

In loving memory of Keith Wilson

7/24/1966 - 07/22/2022

BRITNEYSAMUEL

Sleep in Peace Daddy

THEM OR ME?

Luke 14:26 "If anyone comes to me and does not hate father and mother, wife and children, brothers and sisters—yes, even their own life—such a person cannot be my disciple. 27 And whoever does not carry their cross and follow me cannot be my disciple."

Coming from a background of doing everything with my family, this season of my life was one of the most hardest seasons ever. I was at a crossroads between God and my family and friends . But I had to make a decision, and I had to make one fast. I had no other choice, but to give God my yes, which unknowingly included me being separated from my family. It started with my friends, there was a disconnection between us. No matter how hard we tried to hold on to our relationship my spirit became more and more uneasy. At this point I knew this was God pulling me away from these childhood relationships. These were 10 plus year old relationships that were valued and extremely important to me. I looked at them as if they were my family because they truly were. They were a part of my journey when I was living a lukewarm lifestyle. Many of these relationships were built from trauma bonding but it was time for me to heal. God had to separate me to elevate me and push me to rediscover who I was in the Kingdom of Heaven.

I remember having a conversation with my mom and telling her how uneasy I used to feel when I was around certain individuals and I remember her mentioning to me that I was spiritually sensitive at that time, and that I had to listen to the Holy Spirit not even realizing that my family were the next ones I had to also separate myself from.

During is painful season of separation from my family and my friends there were many things that God revealed to me about one of the issues I struggled with. This was codependency. I took notice that this was something that may have been inherited from both sides of my family because this was something both of my parents also struggled with in their own individual way.

What is codependency?

Codependency in a relationship is when each person involved is mentally emotionally, physically, and/or spiritually reliant on the other.

For me, I struggled with codependency, especially when it came to romantic relationships. I realized that God was separating me from my family to teach me how to find Him on my own. I believe He was also doing the same for my parents so they could learn how to find God in a deeper way on their own. There were many times, and many situations that took place that made me feel like my parents were codependent on me, but when it came to certain things where I needed my parents, I couldn't go to them. I had to deal with alot of my pain and trauma alone because I never felt the level of comfort to be as vulnerable as I could be in front of my parents. During this journey I learned how to run to God for everything and I mean EVERYTHING . I had to learn how to be vulnerable with God, and although it was uncomfortable, it was necessary. One of my favorite scriptures that has kept me going on this journey is Matthew 6:33 and Jeremiah 33:3..

Codependency in my romantic relationships was an epic fail for me . I unfortunately ended up having to learn the hard way over and over again because I had the tendency of giving people too much power over my life . I allowed partners to gain control over me. Their presence had an big impact on my emotions because of the people pleasing spirit that I also had . I

didn't know myself nor did I love myself, so I had the tendency of settling for less than what I deserved all for the sake of not being alone .This was a toxic pattern that had needed to be broken off of me in order for God to shift me into my new.

There was another thing that was revealed to me that I was under. I was under the spirit of witchcraft. I was under the spirit of narcissism, and Jezebel. Witchcraft can show up in many different ways. Rebellion is one of them. According to 1 Samuel 15:23 it says rebellion is like the sin of witchcraft, arrogance like the evil of idolatry.

Going back to rebellion, I know there were many things that my parents were supposed to do that they did not do, and a lot of it had to do with picking up their cross, giving God their full yes, and fulfilling God's purpose for their lives. I know my parents were plagued with fear, the fear of the unknown and many other things but I also know that God trumps it all. On this journey I have learned to choose faith over fear and I have learned to "DO IT SCARED". This is because I understand that according to scripture Hebrews 11:6, faith is what pleases the Lord. So when we operate out of fear and reject God's decree, we begin to walk in disobedience which eventually brings on curses on ourselves and on our bloodlines. (Deuteronomy 28)

Once I understood the importance and the power of obedience, I made a decision to follow God and His decrees even when it didn't make sense to me or even to man. Obedience is better than sacrifice.(1Samuel 15:22).

Now let's talk about the spirit of Narcissism. This spirit is about power and control. People with this spirit are manipulative, selfish, lack empathy, has an excessive need for admiration and so much more. Narcissism is a demonic stronghold and it also carry traits similar to the spirit of Jezebel which is all about control, manipulation, intimidation, and domination. The spirit of Jezebel is one who displays insidious, manipulative and evil tendencies to get their way. Any form of control and/or manipulation is considered witchcraft.

The Bible talks about witchcraft as the work of the flesh "Galatians 3:1". The essence of witchcraft is to control and dominate. This is why Paul said "who" has bewitched you that you don't believe the right thing anymore.

Witches want to control the church, family, and anyone. The means of witchcraft is by intimidation and manipulation. But the ultimate end aim is to dominate and control the child of God.

Domination -to control or have a lot of influence over someone or something, especially in an unpleasant way

Intimidation -the action of frightening or threatening someone, usually in order to persuade them to do something that you want them to do:

Manipulation -. 1. behavior designed to exploit, control, or otherwise influence others to one's advantage

I never knew that I was under these spirits until God pulled me away. You know the famous saying "you can't smell the poo until you're out of it ". God had to separate me so he could show me the healing and deliverance that I needed to receive.

It didn't make sense until a year later as to why I was removed from my family. I had to trust God and trust the process. I remember telling my mom that I had to walk this journey alone, and that later she will understand which is similar to when Jesus mentioned this in John 1:37. I never experienced so much pain from walking away from my parents whom I love so dearly. They couldn't understand it neither, but I had to be obedient.

When walking away from my family I experienced smear campaigns, I was talked about very harshly, there were rumors about me being called crazy and out of my mind (2 Corinthians 5:13-, If we are "out of our mind," as some say, it is for God; if we are in our right mind, it is for you.)

I was called mean and evil, because "you're not supposed to do that to family . You're not supposed to cut your family off. You're letting the enemy use and so much more ".

"Luke 12:51 Suppose ye that I am come to give peace on earth? I tell you, Nay; but rather division:

52   For from henceforth there shall be five in one house divided, three against two, and two against three.

53   The father shall be divided against the son, and the son against the father; the mother against the daughter, and the daughter against the mother; the mother in law against her daughter in law, and the daughter in law against her mother in law."

Before knowing that everything that God was doing was biblical, all of these things that my family were saying to me had me at a point where I was questioning God himself.

He kept saying it's either me or them, and kept referencing me back to two particular scriptures.

"Matthew 19:29 And everyone who has left houses or brothers or sisters or father or mother or wife[a] or children or elds for my sake will receive a hundred times as much and will inherit eternal life." And Luke 14:26 "If anyone comes to me and does not hate father and mother, wife and children, brothers and sisters—yes, even their own life—such a person cannot be my disciple."

There were times my parents would reach out to me, sending long paragraphs condemning me for distancing myself and sometimes I would either not respond or I would simply respond with Love by telling him that I love them. There were even times where I had to send them scripture Luke 14:26 to help them understand that this wasn't my doing . I Thought they would understand but unfortunately they didn't. I knew this time around of me distancing myself from my family was different because I didn't have any hate in my heart towards them. It was simple obedience, and obedience to God was what I was committed to. This was a different kind of pain, but I had to continue to trust God, and lean not to my own understanding. "Proverbs 3:5"

When God gives you instructions, it is a must that you obey his commands. Obedience is better than sacrifice. Obedience brings blessings, disobedience brings curses. Even when we procrastinate and delay what God has instructed us to do it is considered delayed obedience and which is still considered disobedience. Disobedience is as bad as the sin of witchcraft / divination. I encourage you to be committed to pleasing the Lord by your obedience to Him and to stop going out of your way to please man. According to Deuteronomy 28 obedience brings rewards and disobedience brings curses.

So, if you are reading this book, keep going so I can show you how one simple act of obedience has changed my life for the better.

SELF-DISCOVERY:

"Therefore, I urge you, brothers and sisters, in view of God's mercy, to offer your bodies as a living sacrifice, holy and pleasing to God—this is your true and proper worship. 2 Do not conform to the pattern of this world but be transformed by the renewing of your mind. Then you will be able to test and approve what God's will is—his good, pleasing and perfect will." Romans 12:1-2

Christ has always been my foundation. I grew up in church so church is all I knew. My father was an ordained minister and my mother was a prayer warrior. Seeds of Christ was planted in me even as a small child. When I was in elementary school I used to bring the small Bibles to school, I would tell my friends about God during our recess breaks. God was all I knew, and even growing up as an adult although I may have been living a lukewarm lifestyle I was always preaching and teaching the word of God. I use to be out drunk, high on weed, fornicating, cussing, partying, and all, but God was faithfully the topic of my discussions. I grew up around many lukewarm believers so for a season I thought what I was doing was OK. Just as long as I prayed here and there and accepted Christ as my Savior, I just knew that that was my one-way ticket to Heaven. I was so wrong about that and I didn't discover that until I got fully freed from the things of this world.

But before breaking completely free from lukewarm living and idolatry, I got introduced to New Age spirituality.

Here's how it began:

I met someone who I thought was the one. The feelings I had for this person were quite intense. The things I did with him felt so good to my flesh, but I

knew it wasn't right in God's sight. I experienced conviction, but I ran from it because I felt like I "needed" this man in my life. The same spirit that plagued my bloodline came back and showed up in a different way. It was CODEPENDENCY. It was through this situation that I got myself into that became a toxic cycle of intense emotions that left me confused because of the many disappearing acts that he would do.

I used to get so depressed every time he'd up and disappear on me. Until that one day I reached a point of desperation which resorted to me watching tarot. I was desperate for answers so I took the next step and got my first tarot reading. From there on, I became addicted. I was trying to figure out if he was "the one". The more I got lost in tarot was when I started drifting away from God. Scripture tells us to seek ye first the kingdom of God and His righteousness, and all these things will be added, but I was doing the total opposite. Watching tarot led me into a rabbit hole with still many unanswered questions.

Sidenote; if a person comes into your life, and the relationship doesn't push you closer to God, beloved they are NOT the one.

I finally reached a point in my life where enough was enough. I was tired of accepting the bare minimum from this person, so I released him and sent that last goodbye text and SLAMMED that door SHUT. The only problem was, my addiction to new age spirituality did not end there. Three days after closing off that chapter in my life, I was on Facebook and a video of this beautiful black man popped up. I watched that video like 10 times. It felt as though I was looking in the mirror. We spoke the same language and everything. At that time my heart was still closed off because of the disappointment and the heartache. I experience with the past person. I remember promising myself that I would never love another man ever again, and in my mind, I even settled for being the single lady with all of the cats at the end of the block lol. The crazy part is, I don't even like cats, but I was willing to settle for that. Any hews, there was something about this person that I just could not shake. Fast forward, Him and I ended up connecting and this connection felt magical, mysterious and magnetic. We were literally the same person in so many different ways. So of course I had to dig deeper because this connection was something I have never experienced. I begin to do research and look up things like "why does my heart feel certain things being connected to a person and etc. and I ended up seeing things about twin flames. This was a word I've never heard of before, so of course I went to tarot and started indulging in twin flame readings. I became so desperate for answers that I got another reading done. This tarot reading was done by a "twin flame professional". It was over after that lol . Everything turned it into twin flame this twin flame that and as I followed the twin flame readers and videos they spoke a lot about chakra healing. That's when I was introduced to chakras. I was under deep deception that in healing my chakras I would also be healing him as well. It was a mess. Then it turned to me doing actual tarot readings for people and in this season I thought I was doing God's will by walking in purpose but I wasn't. This season didn't last long at all but I do strongly believe that God allowed me to experience this to learn how to hear his voice. One thing I've learned on this journey was to never put God in a box. I also believe he allowed me to experience this season of my life, because through my deliverance, it would help others become delivered and set free as well.

Sidenote: if you are reading this, and you are into tarot, please unsubscribe to it all. You don't need to seek answers from man, nor from these cards. God is able to answer any and all questions that you may have even when it comes to a particular person that you're curious to know if they are ordained for you or not . We are not supposed to rely on anyone or anything but we are called to rely on God. Anything outside of that is idolatry which is considered to be a detestable practice so please, I beg you and I

encourage you to throw those cards away, unsubscribe to those videos, and seek the Father for everything.

I remember when I was into doing tarot readings I heard the voice of the Lord tell me that I'm going to be throwing my cards out really soon. My heart was truly set on pleasing God, so I was open and willing to do whatever He wanted me to do. And then that moment came, he said Brit throw all of those cards, crystals, Palas Santos, and sage in the trash now. He said "you no longer have use for them, I am all that you need". So, guess what I did? I listened and obeyed His voice of instruction and threw out every single item he told me to get rid of .I wasted no time and threw them away immediately.

Once I got rid of them, I started seeing videos on YouTube that talked about ex tarot readers, "how God delivered me from new age "and etc which was even a confirmation for me that I was on the right path. I felt so much peace and excitement because I knew that God had something greater in store for me.

Going back to that special person I still had many questions . So I begin to seek God for answers and through spending time with God, and getting deeper with the Lord, He then showed me and confirmed to me that that person was not a twin flame but that he was actually my God ordained spouse.

The closer I begin to get with the Father, he began to strip me, purge me, purify me and renew my mind. I felt like a brand-new person and that I was. The renewal normally starts with the mind.

This is when he showed me the deception of new age spirituality, and how it was not of God. I went through deliverance, renouncing, denouncing , Fasting and coming out of agreement with new age spirituality. I had officially been rebirthed and sanctified. I made the decision to offer my Body and Soul as a living sacrifice because my desire was to honor, to serve, and to please, the Lord. I realized that new age has played on the emotions of many people who are looking for true love. It was created to become a god in many people's lives, which ends up keeping them away from God, which is The One and only God who can give them the answers that they are searching for.

God is love, and the only way to receiving that love in the physical is through receiving Christ as our first love. Tarot and new age spirituality is a practice that rebels against God's original plan and purpose for our lives. It's like a wolf in sheep's clothing. It promotes peace, love and butterflies, but if you really pay attention, most readers are still single, lonely, and unfulfilled. There is truly no peace, joy, nor happiness in New Age spirituality. No matter how it's presented it still leaves many with a deep void. That void can only be filled through a relationship with Christ Jesus. Since leaving new age, I have truly found my purpose. I have a deeper understanding of who Christ is, and I lack no good thing whether that being spiritually, mentally and emotionally. I have a joy in my spirit that I cannot contain and this is simply from giving God my yes, and not being just a hearer of the word of God, but being also a doer of the word of God.

We serve a jealous God, as scripture says, and the time is now for us to pick a side and not only pick a side, but to stay on it. According to Exodus 20:3 scripture says you shall have no other gods before me.

Self-Reflection:

What are the gods in your life that's keeping you from fully pursuing God's will? Is it money, sex, drugs, new age, people, social media, and/or, etc..?

If it's anyone of these things, I want you to say this prayer with me.

Holy Spirit, I asked you to break any in all connections, known, and even unknown to me that I have with idols or lowercase gods. I asked you to keep them far from me. If I have accepted any gifts that I brought into my home that invites demons or honors force guides out of ignorance, then Lord shine your light on them. I announce, and I announce any, and all idols from my life, and I repent for walking and idolatry, and putting people places and things before you. In Jesus name amen.

Remember this, God has all the answers you need. To receive

wisdom, knowledge and understanding all you have to do is ask him. Learn to be patient and doing so because God always reveals the unhidden things at his appointed time. Scripture says call to me and I will answer you and show you great and mighty things that you have not known. Simply spending time with the father for least, and our daily will truly transform your mind, body and spirit. Get into the habit of running to God before running to anything or anyone else, and I promise you won't be disappointed.

Proverbs 2:3-5

"indeed, if you call out for insight and cry aloud for understanding, and if you look for it as for silver and search for it as for hidden treasure, then you will understand the fear of the Lord and find the knowledge of God."

PASSING OF THE TORCH.

Jeremiah 1:5

**"Before I formed you in the womb I knew[a]
you, before you were born I set you apart;
I appointed you as a prophet to the nations."**

As a child, I've always had a strong spirit of discernment. I always had this, knowing when it came to people, things, and situations. One thing I never asked God was for Him to show me who I was in the kingdom of God. I kind of just knew I was special in some different kind of way lol. I used to have open visions all the time and they would actually play out in the physical. I used to see people's spirit even before personally knowing them. I would have dreams about certain things, and it'd end up playing out in real life.

Until one day… This was the end of April in 2022. I was getting ready for work, got in the shower and I had an open vision of the most disturbing thing I've ever seen in my life.

It was a vision of my father lying in the casket. I asked God what that was, and He spoke these words to me loud and clear. He said, I'm bringing your father home, your mother is going to turn everyone against you and you are not to attend the service", he had told me to stay away. I question God and I

was in disbelief because in my heart, I just knew God wouldn't show nor tell me something like this. He then told me to fast until noon and to read the book of Romans. I called my friend and told her exactly what I seen, I wrote it in my journal, and called my other friend to tell him what I just seen and we were all confused, and lost with words. I finally kind of got myself together and did what the father asked of me to do, and even while experiencing disbelief, uncertainty and despair, a peace came over me. As I sat with the Father and read through Romans ,God explained why it was time to bring Daddy home through that scripture. At that moment, I still questioned it because it was scary knowing this could possibly happen at any given moment. I mourned the loss of my father every night before it actually happened. I was barely able to have a full night's sleep knowing such heartbreaking news could happen any day. One of the worst parts about it was God pulled me into isolation from my family during this season of my life, so it was even harder for me to deal with knowing what God has shown me and not being able to talk to nor be around them. This by far felt like torture. I've always been one to be there for my dad through all of his health issues, so the thought of me not being able to be around if or when this happens really took a toll on me .

My heart shatters even thinking back on this season of my life.

Then, things took a turn, and I got news that my dad was rushed to the hospital. My heart literally fell into my lap. Time went on, and my father's health started to decline. I had an internal fight because I kept hearing God's voice telling me to stay away, but my emotions wanted to come to the rescue as I always did. But again, I had to be obedient and to be honest, I questioned God yet again. I kept asking Him for confirmations if this was truly His will for me to stay away, even knowing Daddy could possibly pass away. Just as soon as I ask God for another confirmation, a video from a young lady on YouTube named Elyse Marie Popped up on my feed. As I began to watch it, at first she was simply talking about her kingdom spouse journey and then she randomly mentioned how God told her that her dad would pass away and how God had also separated her from her family and made her say goodbye to them. When I seen this, I was blown away. I immediately commented on her post to share with her that was currently experiencing the same thing. In that moment I

was even more saddened because I knew that it wasn't just a simple voice in my head telling me, I knew that that voice was and it was Him also preparing me for this moment .As many death scares as my dad has had, death has always been one of my biggest fears for him. The thought of him just being sick really worried me and then to think of him no longer being here always felt like a nightmare.

The very last confirmation God gave me was through another video. I just so happened to stumble across a YouTuber named "Expresswordz", he mentioned the passing of his father in this video as well. I was in total disbelief, because I feel like God was truly preparing me for this moment to come.

Then it happens... I got the call from a friend of the family Friday evening on July 22, 2022, that Daddy had officially transitioned.

My heart dropped. I couldn't think of what to say, nor how to feel . It wasn't registering. I was in disbelief, and although I knew that this moment would come, you can never prepare yourself for death especially the death of a parent. Daddy transitioned two days before his 56th birthday. I was faced with so many different emotions, but I had to push through. I remember laying with God and feeling an unction in my spirit to tell my story to the world as a memorial service for my father via Facebook. I questioned if this was something that I should do so I sought for further clarity and confirmation if this was what God wanted me to do.

I remember going on my dad's Facebook page just to look through his pictures, etc., and I stumbled across a video that my father reposted from Joshua Giles Ministries. I felt led to watch it, but right before watching it, I kept hearing a soft, gentle voice telling me to tell my story, but to be sure I back it up with scripture. During this moment I had an open vision of my dad lying in the hospital bed and getting up from the hospital bed, and walking up the stairs to heaven. As he walked up those stairs, he turned around to look at his body lying on that bed, and then he looked at me and he nodded his head and smiled at me. He then handed me something. Once he handed me that thing, he walked up the stairs to heaven. That open vision had me so emotional because it was such a surreal and vivid vision that also left me with the peace that surpassed my understanding.

I begin watching the video of Pastor Giles speaking on prophetic forecast, and one of the very first things that he mentioned in this video blew my mind.

He mentioned Revelations 4:1 and it read

"After this I looked, and there before me was a door standing open in heaven. And the voice I had first heard speaking to me like a trumpet said, "Come up here, and I will show you what must take place after this."

When he read this scripture, tears begin to flow down my face because this was parallel to the vision I just had about my father walking up the stairs to heaven. It also brought much comfort to me because I knew Daddy made it to heaven.

Not only did that happen, but in that same video Pastor Giles also mentioned one of the very things my father used to always tell me when it came to me making videos, and that was to be sure to back it up with scripture. I was in awe because I literally heard that that very morning when I was trying to make a decision if I should share my story to the world about my father's passing. So, I took it as another confirmation that God was giving me the greenlight to go ahead and go live on Facebook to tell my story. I did just that. I went live on Daddy's birthday to share part of my journey to the world about how God revealed that it was time for Daddy to go be with the Lord. It went very well, and I know I made my dad proud. The message wasn't solely focused on the passing of my father, but the message was focused on salvation, and this was something my dad was big on even when he was asked to speak at different engagements.

My dad was a soul winner for Christ. He was passionate for the Lord. He had a heart for the Father, and his mission was preaching and teaching salvation to those whom he had encountered. I truly believe daddy won many souls to the Kingdom of heaven, and although he struggled with some things as we all do, he did his best at accomplishing what he could accomplish by winning souls to the kingdom of Heaven.

Going back to the open vision I had of daddy passing me that thing, through time God revealed to me that my dad had passed me the mantle. He passed the torch, and I had no idea that only months later I would be walking in purpose and working full-time ministry, preaching and teaching the gospel to the nations.

THE BETRAYAL....

"But I tell you, love your enemies and pray for those who persecute you..."

Matthew 5:44

When daddy passed away, I realized how many people truly hated me. I can count on one hand how many people reached out to me to send their condolences. Going back to the Vision that I had of my dad passing away, and hearing the voice of the Lord telling me that my mother would be the one to turn people against me, I never knew the day would come, not only for the passing of my dad but for the ultimate betrayal from my mother. Though I believed God when He told me this, I still had some doubts that this would happen because I just knew my mom out of all people wouldn't do me like that. But it played out just how I heard it and this is when I learned how necessary and important forgiveness truly is.

This was a deep level of pain that I've never experienced in my life. This was a pain that I wouldn't even wish even on my enemy. I had people block me for no reason out of the blue.

I've heard rumors about me where it was said that I was possessed by the devil. I've heard rumors that I was the reason that my dad died because he died of a broken heart "so they say". I even had my own brother tell me that I was dead to him because of whatever lies he was told about me. No one cared enough to reach out to me to even hear my side of the story. This is when I knew, people were pretending to genuinely have love for me my whole entire life . Had it been someone I loved and knew the sincerity and genuineness of their heart I would have been the first one to reach out to see what's really going on, instead of being quick to believe something negative that was said about them.

I couldn't believe how many people believed such lies and slander about me. I even heard that people was told to stay away from me.

I was in complete shock that this was my life and all of this happened all for the sake me walking in obedience to God.

There was so much that I wanted to say and address, but God would not let me say anything. He made me keep silent as he fought for me on this journey that He called me to. I have learned to be slow to anger, and to be slow to speak and to allow God to fight my battles.

Scripture says(Exodus 14:14) " The Lord will fight for you ; you need only to be still" and that is exactly what I did , I kept still.

I had to constantly do heart checks to make sure I was not harboring any unforgiveness in my heart towards these very individuals who I felt had betrayed me.

I realized that I was following the steps of Jesus because he had also experienced betrayal, so this was something that I had to go through to help me become who I am today.

According to scripture, Peter had denied Jesus three times, but Jesus forgave him, and still encouraged him not to give up, and to be strong, and assured of his love for him.

Although there has been a separation within the family dynamic, I still had to learn to forgive them and love them at a distance. Forgiveness is so important on this journey because according to scripture Matthew 6:14 it says for if you forgive other people when they sin against you, your heavenly Father will also forgive you. This scripture holds so much weight because for God to forgive us, we have to forgive others. So it doesn't matter what anyone has done to you or what anyone has said about you ,they are not worth having God not forgive you because you failed to forgive them. They are not worth your blessings being blocked.

Harboring unforgiveness can result in many things and can keep you stagnant in life. It can even cause health issues, so ask yourself what am I holding onto that I need to release? Who do I need to forgive so that God can forgive me?

I want you to always keep in mind that number one, we live in a spiritual world and number two, when anyone does you wrong, we cannot be mad at that individual. We have to learn and recognize that we're not dealing with fleshly things, but against the rulers, against the authorities, against the powers of this dark world, and against the spiritual forces of evil, and the heavily realms .

So, whenever you're facing opposition from the enemy, put on the full armor of God, because again, we're not fighting fleshly things and in knowing this, we must keep in mind that we cannot win spiritual battles with our flesh. We can only win spiritual battles with the Holy Spirit, which is why it's important to put on the full armor of God daily and to anoint yourselves daily. The enemy is here to steal, kill, and destroy, and we have to be equipped enough to beat him as his own game.

This season of betrayal also taught me what love truly is according to the word of God.

Scripture says, love is patient, love is kind. It does not envy, it does not boast, it is not proud. It does not dishonor others, it is not self-seeking, it is not easily angered, it keeps no records of wrongs. Love does not delight in evil, but rejoices with truth. It always protects always trust, always hopes, always persevere.

Most of those who I felt betrayed by, did not operate in any of these characteristics according to a word of God. What I learned about love is that it's unconditional and it's not based off how "I can control you". As mentioned, love protects, and through this season, my name, my character, and my image was not protected.

Because I had decided to give God my yes, it unfortunately created enemies that were even in my own household.

(Matthew 10:36-Your enemies will be right in your own

household!')

But guess what? I forgive them all and I pray daily for their deliverance and salvation.

I encourage you, as scripture Matthew 5:44 mentions to love your enemies and pray for those who persecute you .

One other important scripture is Matthew 18:21-22 Then Peter came to Jesus and asked, "Lord, how many times shall I forgive my brother or sister who sins against me? Up to seven times?"

Jesus answered, "I tell you, not seven times, but seventy-seven times.

What does this mean?

This means, we are to forgive over and over and over again. If we are called to be disciples of Christ, then we are called to do these very things that Jesus has done. He set the example for us to follow His teachings and His steps.

Remember we are not about being just hearers of the word of God, but we are called to be doers of the word of God.

THE BIRTH OF TRUST, OBEY & IMAGINE MINISTRIES.

Trust : Proverbs 3:5-6 5 "Trust in the Lord with all your heart and lean not on your own understanding in all your ways submit to him, and he will make your paths straight."

Obey : 1 Samuel 15:22 "Obedience is better than sacrifice."

Imagine : 1 Corinthians 2:9 "But as it is written: "Eye has not seen, nor ear heard, Nor have entered into the heart of man The things which God has prepared for those who love Him.""

This season is when my life took a complete and unexpected turn.

I was employed with LabCorp for seven years. I started out as doing accessioning and transitioned to drawing blood and then to working Client Services over the phone.

When Covid hit, many of LabCorp's employees got sent home to work from home. This was almost like a dream come true because I've been wanting to work from home for a long time but my performance didn't allow it. This was the season where I made my first "big girl" move. I had left my ex-husband (which is a really good friend now and a wonderful father) and I got my first starter-up apartment as a single mother. On top of that I had a nice paying job which allowed me to work out of the comfort of my own home.

Even though I was excited about this new life, I still felt like something was missing. I worked full-time for LabCorp and I had a couple of side jobs as well but for some strange reason it seemed like I couldn't keep money in my pockets.

There was no dramatic change in my finances, in fact, I had a couple of raises, but my money still wasn't showing for anything. Then I started noticing the extra pressure and the extra micromanagement that was taking place on the job, even with me working from home. I wasn't feeling it all!

Every day, I would ask God what my purpose was, but I didn't realize until later that he was actually transforming my life into the very thing He called me to do. Everything on the job began to feel super uncomfortable. Even after the passing of my dad, things began to take a turn for the worse. I felt that my name was being talked about amongst other employees at my job. Everything about the job started being extra weird to me, even down to the people. One day one of my calls got pulled by my supervisor, and it was a particular call where I had a patient on hold for a long time, (yea I know lol) and my supervisor was able to see that I was pulling up Bible scriptures on the work computer. So of course, I got called into a meeting and got in trouble. But for some odd reason, I honestly did not care. I remember my boss saying to me "maybe this is not the field that you should be working in" and I agreed and ended up saying to my boss that I would choose to save somebody's life any day over taking a call for LabCorp. I told my boss to do what she got to do because she kept threatening me that she was going to take this call to HR and then kept mentioning that "I needed this job". I ended up saying to her "I don't need this job, As long as I got God I'm good". I can't even lie, there was such a boldness that came over me during this meeting that I shocked my own self and that's only because I used to be the one saying that "I need my job", but in this particular moment, I was confident in knowing that I didn't need that job, and that all I had needed was God. Around that same time, I remember saying to myself "I'm about to quit this job". I felt it so strong in my spirit that it was time for me to quit this job, but I was still fearful. I was still trying to plan a backup plan in case I had decided to randomly quit the job instead of me simply allowing God to be my back up plan. I remember even after having that call, in my mind I was determined to do something to make them fire me (PETTY BETTY) because I wasn't quitting and that was on period lol. I knew the rule for unemployment was t if you quit your job, you would not qualify for any unemployment benefits, so I say OK Ima make them fire me just so I can get a check. But God said NOPE you're not going to make me look bad.

Trust Obey Imagine Ministries was officially birthed September 20, 2022.

On this day, I remember getting ready for work and at this time I was working full-time for LabCorp as a client services representative. I was in the shower, and I heard the spirit of the Lord tell me to put my resignation letter in and that He wants me to go full-time into ministry. When I heard this I instantly questioned it. I wasn't sure if it was my own thoughts or if it was the Holy Spirit. In this season of my life, I was still getting familiar with God's voice. The only time that I confidently experienced God's voice so clear was when He told me that my dad would pass away. So, hearing this really had me questioning myself because this is something that I would have never done on my own will. I was a newly divorced single mother of three that worked full-time for LabCorp. I had a few side hustles, and I never had to depend nor rely on anyone financially so the thought of leaving my 9-5 was a complete shock to me because in my mind, "WHAT AM I GONNA DO?". How am I going to pay my bills? How am I going to be able to take care of my children? All of these things started to come up, so I tried to shake the thought, but it was pressing on my spirit SO INTENSLEY that I knew for certain that it was coming from God. I Instead of continuously fighting the thoughts, I asked God for several confirmations. He gave me about four different confirmations, but of course I still wasn't fully convinced. Until later on that day, my daughter Britain came home from school. Sis came straight to my room, and she said" mom I think God wants me to tell you this. I've never felt this before, but God told me to tell you that you have to quit your job". The moment she said that I felt my stomach fall into my lap! At that point there was no more confirmations needed because HOW is this even possible? I didn't tell my kids about any of what the father told me, so the fact that she came home and told me this was mind blowing. Right after she said this to me, she said mom look at the clock and the time was 3:33pm.

Back then I didn't know what 333 meant but just looking back it makes a lot of sense as to why God showed me that number after receiving the confirmation from my daughter.

Jeremiah 33:3 says, "Call to me and I will answer you and tell you great and unsearchable things you do not know.'

God was simply giving me the answer to my question through my daughter Britain.

I HAD to be obedient. He used my child to confirm the revelation and it was NO more running from it. All doubt had left the building.

One thing that I learned on this journey is, sometimes God will not move until you move. So, we may be waiting for a breakthrough, but a lot of times, God may be simply waiting for us to take that step so that He can meet us right half way.

According to James 2:14-18 Scripture says "What good is it, my brothers and sisters, if someone claims to have faith but has no deeds? Can such faith save them? Suppose a brother or a sister is without clothes and daily food. If one of you says to them, "Go in peace; keep warm and well fed," but does nothing about their physical needs, what good is it? In the same way, faith by itself, if it is not accompanied by action, is dead.

But someone will say, "You have faith; I have deeds."

Show me your faith without deeds, and I will show you my faith by my deeds."

So guess what I did y'all? I turned that resignation letter in, and to be honest, I thought I was losing my mind. I was scared as ever because this is something that I've never done before. Like who just quits jobs without having a backup plan? Lol. I've always been one that had a job, and had that whole "miss independent woman" mindset. I felt like my security blanket got stripped away from me. But I had to be obedient and show God I had faith in Him by my deeds.

In my mind, I decided that that's what I was going to do. I was going to quit my job and type up my resignation letter. Before the end of my work shift God dropped the name of my ministry in my spirit! He led me to scriptures to support the name of the ministry which is mentioned in the beginning of this chapter.

I wasn't sure how this was going to play out but I was in complete surrender to Gods will .

Fear started to arise and I started to question God like "Lord how am I going to do this?" I kept hearing Him say over and over "Do you trust me or not" ?

Fast forward,

On October 14, 2022, Trust, Obey, Imagine Ministries was publicly released. This day was the day I aired my first YouTube video. For those who have been with me since the beginning of this journey, most of you know that my backdrop was a boat. This boat was a symbolization of a spiritual journey on the sea of life. A boat without a pilot is lost. God guides the souls journey. It also symbolizes transport, a means of travel within a spiritual world. The boat can also mean to carry the souls of the dead to heaven. I also look at it as carrying the souls of the spiritually dead to the throne of heaven. This boat symbolizes the vehicle of faith, trust, and grace to support this courageous journey.

It represents the kingdom of Christ and His followers. Going back to when Jesus told his disciples to follow me and I will make you fishers of men .

What are fishers of men? Fishers of men are spiritual quickened men who are strongly fortified in truth and able to help others find the light. It also means to be the light that draws those who are caught in the waves of darkness.

I created the YouTube platform. I set up the email and created an Instagram all by faith and obedience.

I wanted to show the Father through my deeds that I was serious about this thing.

I had ordered my backdrop and set up my little space in my living room for when I go live and stuff. Sis was ready to work!

Here's a quick back story:

One day I started running low on funds and I instantly went into hustle/survival mode. So, I decided to go out to door dash. I remember sitting at a red light on Kirkwood highway near Cleveland avenue in Newark Delaware and I heard the Lord say to me, you are on my payroll now . I didn't call you out of your job to still work for man, you work for me." And when I heard Him say payroll, I looked to the left of me and there was a billboard that had the word "Payroll" written big and bold. I was like WOW! I hear you Lord. But of course, I proceeded with my door dash order.

I barely made money that day, so I decided to go out the next day to do a Amazon run. I got to the Amazon, grabbed a cart and loaded my car up with packages. It took forever for me to get done, I was so irritated and hot and OVER it lol. Once I finished, I hop in my car to start the car and guess what? The car completely died out. On top of that, my phone was also dying so in that moment I knew it was God slapping me on my hand because I was being disobedient. I was stuck and stranded for almost 2 hours at the amazon warehouse. My mechanic ended up coming to my rescue "Thank God" and days later, my check engine light came on and it never went off (even up until the day my car got repossessed). God was speaking so loudly! He wanted to make sure I understood His assignment for my life. He did NOT want me to work for nobody but Him.

After those setbacks, it was safe to say that I fully understood the assignment!! I said you know what Lord; I surrender my all to you.

From then on, I've been working full time for the Lord.

The Lord gave me my first message to put out on YouTube on October 14, 2022. When I put it out, I felt pretty good about it and was super excited. The Father kept telling me to just stay consistent. I only put messages out when He led me to so it wasn't an everyday thing but, I was still consistent with writing down my revelations.

I remember randomly putting out a message titled PUSH! This message was not rehearsed nor written out. This was a Holy Spirit led message that came straight from the throne. This video was the first video that I've ever done that went viral! I went from 23 subscribers to like 700 subscribers within a very short time span. Day by day my ministry began to grow. It was nothing but the Lord breathing on it. As I'm typing, I'm at 10k subscribers and it hasn't even been two full years! This is a true example of God putting his super on your natural. From then on, the ministry has grown and changed thousands of lives and it is STILL thriving. Only God can do something like this, and He gets all of the glory, honor and praise.

Learning how to surrender control is a very uncomfortable experience but it is necessary. We must keep in mind that we don't belong to ourselves BUT that we belong to God. So, it is best to fully surrender to Gods will so that we can receive the fullness of what He has in store for us.

Scripture says "Many are the plans in a person's

heart, but it is the Lord's purpose that prevails.

(Proverbs 19:21)

A lot of times we make plans for our lives and future which

doesn't include God. We tend to think that our plans are what's best for us not realizing that it's only Gods plans that's best for us and prevails over ours.

"Jeremiah 29:11 For I know the plans I have for you," declares the LORD, "plans to prosper you and not to harm you, plans to give you hope and a future."

I thought I had a plan for my life but the moment I surrendered to His will, all of my plans melted away and God changed the whole trajectory of my life. He changed my life in a way I could have never imagined.

Isaiah 55:8-9 "For my thoughts are not your thoughts, neither are your ways my ways," declares the Lord.

9 "As the heavens are higher than the earth, so are my ways higher than your ways and my thoughts than your thoughts."

God had me rip up my back up plans (Amazon & DoorDash) and instead of me hustling and chasing money He taught me how to seek Him first so all of His goodness can flow to me.

Society has many of us chasing the bag and then forgetting about Christ.

When the real truth is when we seek Him, then the bag will chase us ." Matthew 6:33 But seek ye first the kingdom of God, and his righteousness; and all these things shall be added unto you." When serving, obeying and following His commands, the blessings comes to us .

Scripture says" Proverbs 10:22 the blessings of the Lord maketh rich and adds no sorrow "

These are heavenly blessings that we don't have to toil and labor for. These are blessings and rewards given to us due to our obedience to the Lord.

All it takes is a revelation to shift your perspective and your life will never be the same. I have learned the true definition and importance of surrendering to Gods will, letting go of complete control, and having faith in the impossible. I pray that this testimony shifts your perspective and encourages you to always partner with God so that he can make any and all crooked paths straight. Remember to Trust in the Lord and not lean to your own understanding, to obey his voice of instruction and to imagine the impossible because when God is breathing on it all things are possible.

Walking in obedience and fully trusting in the Lord and not leaning into my own understanding was probably the biggest faith test I've ever had to experience.

I know I looked crazy to many people, and I felt pretty crazy, but I had to push past those thoughts and those voices and move in obedience, no matter how uncomfortable it felt. Coming from being newly single to having three kids with no other financial means of support, to having to fully rely on God for my bread and my butter was super super scary. But one thing I can say is, since taking this leap of faith, I have experienced God in the most supernatural way. On this walk, He has shown me that He is my provider, He is my protector, and lastly that He is a promise keeper. He promised that he would never leave me nor forsake me, and I'm so honored to say that He hasn't told one lie EVER!

I have seen God perform miracles, countless of times on this journey and to be quite honest, the lifestyle that I live doesn't even make sense on paper. I've had people tell me that they've never heard of anything like my story before. This journey is truly miraculous. I've never felt so loved, so provided for, so protected, so comforted, and fulfilled not even from man as I do from the Lord. No one could ever compare to His unfailing love and protection. I am so in love with my Heavenly Father, and I do not regret listening to that small still voice telling me to leave my job to go full time into ministry. I'm choosing faith over fear any day because I've witnessed too many miracles from walking by faith.

One of the many things that we can do to please the Lord is to show our faith in Him by our actions. Scripture tells us that faith is what pleases the Lord. If God is telling you to do a particular thing, even if it's leaving your job, writing that book, starting that business, starting that podcast, or
whatever it may be, as long as you're walking in obedience and putting God first, He will surely breathe on it.

Release all fear, and do not worry too far ahead of you. Learn to take it day by day and to be present. Let tomorrow worry about itself. Scripture says how many of you worrying can add a single hour to your life.

Remember this, God is the God of faith, and the enemy is the god of fear. Who do you truly serve?

I Encourage you to trust in the Lord with all your heart and lean not to your own understanding. I encourage you to stop trying to figure it out and just do it. Do it scared.

In all that you're doing, do it for the Lord and be joyful in doing so.

Remember that obedience is everything and anything that you do for the Lord will be blessed 1000-fold in return. Do not make God force you into doing His will because that's when it will become super uncomfortable. Instead, surrender to His will and He will reward you.

WALKING ON WATER.

Deuteronomy 11:11

New International Version

"But the land you are crossing the Jordan to take possession of is a land of mountains and valleys that drinks rain from heaven."

Can I be honest with you?

I never knew that there were different levels of the promised land until I experienced it for myself.

I've learned about Jesus sending out his disciples to disciple the lost sheep but I never knew I would be living it.

On March 17, 2023, this was the date that my lease was up. God told me months ago that I would not be renewing my lease, neither did he tell me where I would be moving to.

On this day, we said goodbye to what we knew to be "our normal life ". I was sent destiny helpers to help me pack up my home and move me out of it. God was speaking loudly about Texas but to be completely honest I knew I

wasn't ready for Texas yet. God knew that also and this is where life and discipleship really began.

The very last day of living there, my children and i sat around waiting for God to give me details of where he wants me to go. It was at the very last minute that it was revealed. This is unexpected and confusing all at the same time. He led me and my 3children to Ramada hotel. Boy was I angry at God. I had a temper tantrum out of this world because for starters, God was giving me revelation that I was going to my KS house to dwell there or so I thought. But I guess it wasn't time yet. This is where my season of processing really began.

I was blessed to be able to afford hotel living (and it is NOT CHEAP). I filed my taxes from that previous year, and it came on time, so money wasn't an issue for me. It was just the fact that I had no home. How humbling is that right? I didn't allow the situation to steal my joy, so the kids and I made the best out of the circumstances and learned how to be content even with the little. It was a learning experience for me personally because I had to learn how to detach from materialistic things and learn to be joyful and happy even without the things I was used to having. In this season of processing, I learned just because you may lack certain things materialistically that it doesn't define who you are. When you have Jesus, you lack no good thing. So, whether I had a home or not, I had Jesus and I had a peace that surpassed my understanding. Having that alone is priceless.

Fast forward, I thought it was quite interesting because the end of my lease was 3/17/23. I like to reference 317 to Joshua 3:17

The priests who carried the ark of the covenant of the LORD stopped in the middle of the Jordan and stood on dry ground, while all Israel passed by until the whole nation had completed the crossing on dry ground."

In my mind, when I left my home, I thought I was crossing over into my promised land. It didn't look like it nor did it feel like it. But I had a shift in perspective and realized that I truly was living in my promise land.

When funds began to get low, I was surviving off of Mannah. It was supernatural how God was providing for me and my family. I would receive help from my ministry and then at times people would randomly pour into me to support my journey. The lifestyle I was living did not make sense on paper at all and I was truly living in the supernatural. I had good days and I had bad days and at times my faith struggled because I was tired and longed for a place to call home. This was me fully walking on water, and I knew that if I

looked back I would be forfeiting everything God has promised me. Not only that, but I would be letting so many people down that were also on a similar journey and/or being called to this journey and I couldn't do that. I wanted to show the world how real God is and how He miraculously provides for us when we surrender to His will when completely walking away Egypt.

The time came for us to leave this hotel. I was completely unsure of our next move, but I had to leave in obedience. This was about 2months later of us living at the Ramada inn.

For those 2 months, I felt like I went through intense healing, deliverance and training which had required a period of isolation and consecration. I believe during that season God was preparing me to be sent out to disciple.

The next stop was a friend of mine who was also supporting and walking with me on this journey. She opened her home to us plenty of times before but every time she did, I turned it down because it didn't make sense to me to go there. It seemed pointless to go live with someone when I could've just renewed my lease or simply searched for a new home to live. So the time had come and once again she opened up her home to us . Money was super funny at that time and I didn't have enough to get another room so I knew God allowed me to be out of all options just so I can swallow my pride and go live with my friend.

I remember getting a call from my beautiful prophetic cousin Tova and the conversation led to her softly rebuking me and telling me to go down there to my friends house . So (rolling my eyes) lol I listened and humbled myself and drove down there. She lived about an hour away from me and it was completely away from everything I was used to.

She welcomed us in with love and then as time went on, God revealed that it was time for me to go but first I had to complete my assignment while I was there. I honestly wasn't sure what my assignment was so I let time pass and allowed for it to be revealed. One day my friend asked for some prophetic advice for her own personal journey so I opened the Bible and just allowed the Holy Spirit to speak and flow through me . In that moment, my assignment was revealed. He wanted me to convert her back to Christ.

Every single scripture lead to him revealing that it was time for her to pick a side and return fully to the Lord. Sis understood the assignment and began to repent and denounce the Muslim faith and decided to dedicate her life back to Christ and serve the Lord.

After that happened, I went to my room and I heard the Lord say "mission accomplished, now it's time to go" . He then took me to a scripture to confirm what He said and I was in complete shock.

"Joshua 22:1 Then Joshua summoned the Reubenites, the Gadites and the half-tribe of Manasseh 2 and said to them, "You have done all that Moses the servant of the Lord commanded, and you have obeyed me in everything I commanded. 3 For a long time now—to this very day—you have not deserted your fellow Israelites but have carried out the mission the Lord your God gave you"

During this revelation he kept showing me 319 which in Strongs Hebrew means the afterpart, end so I knew my time of being there came to an end .

Not long after that I left her house and went back to a living in a hotel. In that season it was reveal to me that He sent me there to disciple just how Matthew 10 describes it .

Matthew 10:5These twelve Jesus sent out with the following instructions: "Do not go among the Gentiles or enter any town of the Samaritans. 6 Go rather to the lost sheep of Israel. 7 As you go, proclaim this message: 'The kingdom of heaven has come near.' 8 Heal the sick, raise the dead, cleanse those who have leprosy,[a] drive out demons. Freely you have received; freely give.

9 "Do not get any gold or silver or copper to take with you in your belts— 10

no bag for the journey or extra shirt or sandals or a staff, for the worker is worth his keep. 11 Whatever town or village you enter, search there for some worthy person and stay at their house until you leave. 12 As you enter the home, give it your greeting. 13 If the home is deserving, let your peace rest on it; if it is not, let your peace return to you. 14 If anyone will not welcome you or listen to your words, leave that home or town and shake the dust off your feet.

Through time God was making it more and more clear that I am living the life of a disciple. Most of the disciples had no home, they were homeless and sent to gather the lost sheep, heal, deliver and set the captives free. God began teaching me how to be that fisherman and how to be the light in the midst of darkness. This was an assignment that I had no idea I would be on, but because I gave to Lord my yes I had, to allow him to lead and direct my path.

Now I'm back in a hotel, but this time I'm at another hotel. This was an "Extended stay of America. I had two particular assignments here at that location and each time I had to walk in the boldness of the Lord and speak whatever God led me to speak to who he assigned me to speak to. God was still providing and paying my bills and lodging expenses as I was ministering to the world and completing the assignments He called me to. The people who worked at this hotel favored me and genuinely cared for me and spoke highly of me. It was truly a wonderful experience even when I had my bad days.

Fast forward the time has come for me to leave this place. We were there for several months, and God was showing me for some time that I would be leaving there soon. He kept telling me to stay packed up. It got to a point where I got frustrated because every time He told me to pack up, I would pack but I never went anywhere. I was so tired of it and started growing weary.

So, one day I said to God, if it's time for me to leave this time then I ask that you provide more than enough funds for me to buy suitcases. Guess what? The next day I was blessed, and I was able to buy suitcases. Weeks later I tried to pay to extend my room and all of the rooms were sold completely out! I knew God was pushing me up out of there. He kept giving me revelations about me leaving soon so when this happened, I knew it was God shifting us. We ended up packing everything up and found a super low rate at the Hilton. I was like ummmm ok Lord this makes no sense. So, we went to the Hilton and stayed only two nights there. When I pulled up to Hilton to park the car, there was a car that was parked directly behind me that had a license plate from Texas. I didn't think nothing of it because it just seemed too far off, so I continued on my way. Then the time came for us to leave this place. I was led to the Embassy suites by Hilton and this hotel had an indoor swimming pool so I thought it was pretty dope because I wanted my kids to freely enjoy themselves. Once I pulled up to this hotel, there was a white truck parked in front of me that also had a Texas license plate. I begin to question if this was my next move. Things began to happen, doors started to shut in on me, and I was under attack that week, and I just couldn't understand why. I remember having a conversation with my sis in Christ and she said to me, Sis, you may be going to Texas sooner than you think. I didn't fully come into agreement with what she said because again it just didn't make sense to me. I knew my circumstances; I knew I didn't have money for Texas and I honestly didn't feel as though I was ready to just get up and leave like that. Then the next day, my bro in Christ called me and he ended up saying the same exact thing to me. He said Sis ,yesterday when we were on the phone I kept hearing Texas over and over and he said I apologize because I should've said it then. He basically confirmed what my sis previously mentioned to me. And I still wasn't receiving it because again, how am I going to get to Texas with no money and no car. So I sat with the Lord, and I specifically asked Him about Texas. I asked Him what part of Texas He wants me to go to and if it's time for me to go to Texas, I asked him to provide the funds to get me there. I had a moment of crying out from the depths of my soul to the Lord for help. I ended up posting on my YouTube community post and this was the most vulnerable I have ever been in my life. I felt like giving up and just going back to my old life. I literally was out of all options and all I could do is lay there and cry out to God.

That very next morning after going through so much warfare, so much doubt, so many emotions, and even fear I had received one of the biggest breakthroughs of my life that I knew only God could do. I received confirmation that God wanted me to go to Houston Texas asap, and I

had also received more than enough funds to book me and my children a one-way flight to Houston Texas. We were also blessed with enough money for us to book a hotel for about a week for when we arrive to Houston.

I knew this was a window that probably wouldn't come back around if I missed this opportunity. So, by faith, I booked those tickets, and we left that next day and the process of getting to the airport and even down to the plane ride was nothing but God. We were shown so much favor. This was my youngest kids first time on the plane and they were even blessed to take a picture with the pilot and able to chill out in the cockpit area. This is when I realized that we had crossed over onto another level of our promised land. When we got here, I've encountered miracles after miracles after miracles. The hotel that we first went to, the young lady that works as a general supervisor said she knew me from social media, and that she was a follower on TikTok. This was nothing but God. I ended up meeting another young lady that I've been connected to through my ministry, and she ended up living about 20 minutes away from where I was staying. She even came over and we met each other for the first time in person. I cooked for her, and we fellowshipped and she mentioned how she specifically prayed to God for Him to send me to Houston Texas because she was in need of a sister in Christ that is like-minded. This move was an answered prayer for her. I then met another young lady who's been following my Trust Obey Imagine Ministries who came and did my hair free of charge. This is an example of divine connections and being at the right place at the right time. It is so much more I can testify to that has happened since being here . Since being here God has been showing me the physical manifestations that this is where I'm supposed to be.

Right now, I am still walking on water and believing God for my new home. I know I will soon testify, but as of now, we are still living daily by faith and fulfilling what God has called me to do.. No matter how difficult it may get, God will continue to get the glory, and I vow to never look back.

To be continued.

SOMETIMES YOU HAVE TO LOSE, TO WIN AGAIN !

"Whoever finds their life will lose it, and whoever loses their life for my safe will find it."

Matthew 10:39

In all that I've lost I'm realizing more and more that God has removed things from my life because the things that I acquired was not acquired with him. I'm learning more and more that He is destroying faulty foundations and that He wants everything new for us. I had a dream about a house being caught on fire, and I remember in the dream it was a pastor having a fit because of this house being on fire and I remember walking up to the Pastor saying to him. Sometimes you must let it burn down in order for God to rebuild it.

On this journey, I lost a lot. I had to walk away from a lot, but I know it was for a greater purpose. I have learned that everything that was done without God is being destroyed, which includes homes, marriages, cars, jobs, friendships, and God is rebuilding it all from scratch and on a firm foundation which is Christ Jesus whom is our cornerstone.

One thing that I've lost which I haven't really mentioned was my car. I'm only making mention of this because I know and feel in my spirit that I am coming back with another update and testimony of how God got me the car He desires for me. I had lexy for 4 whole years and I prayed to God to allow me to pay her off but He had other plans and I trust that He knew best. I lost my car in the middle of February of 2024. It was a bitter sweet moment because on one hand I was relieved of the stress of having that car but on the other hand , it was upsetting because not only was I homeless but I was also car-less. I was trying my very best to hold onto lexy but God had other plans. It felt like the Father was providing just enough for me to be able to afford food, lodging expenses and other miscellaneous things. The stress of the car note became too much for me and I had no other choice but to surrender that vehicle to Him. The check engine light wouldn't go off, the other lights on the dashboard were coming on. Man, it just felt like poor lexy was falling apart. The crazy part about it was it was still a beautiful and fairly new car. I tried trading the car in and I couldn't. It was more of a burden to keep the car. Once I made the decision to surrender the car to God, I began seeing tow trucks EVERYWHERE!! I was honestly stressed out because I felt that the repo man was going to show up sooner than later. And surely it did! I was so shocked that they was able to locate me at the hotel that I was staying in and that hotel was located in the cut. All I seen was red lights in front of the hotel window in the middle of the night and the tow truck was taking my car. I instantly jumped up and ran outside. By the time I got out to the car, I noticed that the car was parked in the middle of the street and the tow truck was up the street. The truck turned around and came back towards my car. The guy got out of his tow truck and was super kind and allowed me to get all of stuff out of the car. It was as if God stopped them from taking my car just so I can catch him to get the rest of my belongings. I honestly didn't know how to feel, but I will say that kept a straight face and pushed back my tears and told God "Lord I trust you".

But just thinking back, God knew what He was doing because where He was taking me , He knew my car wouldn't get me there.

I have lost a lot of materialistic things, but what I've gained is a real true, intimate relationship with God and a peace that man could never give me, so if you ask me would I sacrifice it all, I will do it over and over and over again. I have lost sisterhoods and different relationships on this journey and it was very painful and confusing at first but God promises us restoration . He always restores it back with better. Not saying that anyone is better than anyone but what I can say is the relationships that God has restored me with are God ordained relationships where Christ is the foundation. I no longer have relationships where trauma is the foundation. I walked away from my job to follow Christ, but what I've gained is identity in Christ, I gained purpose, I gained wisdom, and I gained a passion for Christ more than I've ever have. So in all actuality, although I had to leave my job, I really didn't lose anything. If anything, I gained ALOT. One of the biggest things that I've gained in losing is freedom. I am no longer a slave to this world, but I am now a slave to Christ, which equates to freedom and liberty.

"2Corinthian 3:17 Now the Lord is the Spirit, and where the Spirit of the Lord is, there is freedom."

When God gives you new, He has to also remove the old. We have to learn how to trust the process when God is removing certain things, people, places, etc. from our lives because it's all for the good of the Lord. Scripture says.

"2 Corinthians 5:17-

Therefore, if any man be in Christ, he is a new creature: old things are passed away; behold, all things are become new"

Once we are in Christ, the old things no longer exist. They are now a thing of the past and everything in your life will be made new. So, when God removes things, I want you to understand that He is simply making room for your new. Sometimes we are still connected to things That are connected to the things in the world. This could be people, places, or things, and we must allow God to destroy those connections because in all actuality, those things are sometimes things that keeps us bound. For God to give us new, we must let go of the baggage, and letting go of the baggage requires us to open our hands to receive what God has for us. If we're still holding on to those things, it's impossible to open our hands to receive what God has for us because we're too busy having our hands closed off from carrying that deadweight.

If God is telling you to let something go understand that He is not telling you to let it go to punish you, but He's telling you to let these things go so that He can bless you with better.

Think back on Jobs story, he lost everything, but God restored him with so much more. God restored Jobs fortunes and He gave him twice as much as he had before and so in the same way God did this for Job, just know that he will do it for you.

"Job 42:10

After Job had prayed for his friends, the Lord restored his fortunes and gave him twice as much as he had before."

God promises us beauty for our ashes and joy for our pain, so know that in all that you have lost, and all that you have suffered, and all that you have endured that God is going to give you double for your trouble, but no matter what you have to keep going.

"Isaiah 61:3

and provide for those who grieve in Zion— to bestow on them a crown of beauty instead of ashes, the oil of joy instead of mourning, and a garment of praise instead of a spirit of despair. They will be called oaks of righteousness, a planting of the LORD for the display of his splendor."

Do not throw in a towel even when you feel like your back is against the wall, keep pressing in, keep praying, keep fasting, keep worshiping him because scripture says this:

"Blessed is the one who perseveres under trial because, having stood the test, that person will receive the crown of life that the Lord has promised to those who love him.

James 1:12"

As long as you don't give up, you will win, so I encourage you to keep going no matter what it looks like. Have faith in the impossible and stay in your word. Faith comes by hearing in by hearing the word of God, so whenever you feel like you are faced with trials and tribulations, get into the word of God, sit in the presence of the Lord, and allow him to renew your strength.

This journey reminded me of the title of this song by Fantasia called sometimes you have to lose to win again because I lost it all but what I gained is eternal life, and sometimes you have to do just that in order to truly win.

You're really not winning until you are winning for Christ .

"Matthew 16:25-For whoever wants to save their life will lose it, but whoever loses their life for me will find it."

I am still in between miracles and blessings and so I will keep you posted on what else the Lord does for me and my life but one thing I do know that this is my season restoration and although I'm currently still living in Airbnb and without a vehicle, I know that God has promised me a new EVERYTHING. And I know very soon I will look back on this page and testify of how God's promise came to pass in my life. I encourage you to continue to believe, to continue to have the faith of Abraham. Abraham's promise came by his belief and as i always say ,the keys to receiving is believing. So I encourage you on this day to push. Continue to have faith and know that everything that you are going through is a part of your testimony, and God is working all things out for your good.

I love you. Peace, Love and Blessings.

12 MONTH PREPARATION:
BECOMING HIS BRIDE SNEAK PEAK

Esther 2:12

"Before each young woman was taken to the king's bed, she was given the prescribed twelve months of beauty treatments—six months with oil of myrrh, followed by six months with special perfumes and ointments."

In the previous chapters of this book, I spoke about all the different phases and chapters of my life. All that I have went through during this season was in a 12-month span.

What was revealed to me was God was preparing me for my God ordained spouse.

I underwent healing , deliverance, finding my purpose , walking into purpose , learning how to disciple others , learning what love is according to 1 Corinthians 13:4, learning the fruits of the spirit , learning self-love , learning how to be a proverbs 31 woman , learning how to allow God to lead my life (true surrender), and so much more .

All of these things have been preparing me for what I originally was placed on this journey for, and that is preparation for marriage.

I will be going more into depth later about becoming His bride so please stay tuned.

I'm sorry that this chapter ends here, but I wanted to keep you guys on the edge of your seats. I pray that my story inspires and encourages you to fully live a life for the Lord, and to do it unapologetically.

EPILOGUE: GOD DID IT!

Isaiah 55:11 Niv

"So is my word that goes out from my mouth: It will not return to me empty, but will accomplish what I desire and achieve the purpose for which I sent it."

Just when I thought this book was done being written, God came through for me. He would not let me finish this book without adding this miraculous testimony. I know I mentioned earlier in this book that I was still living in an Airbnb and waiting for God to fulfill His promise of my new home. Well Let me just say, this came by surprise and it came swiftly with the hand of God all over it.

Story time!!

As previously mentioned, God called me to Texas. My family and I were living in Airbnb's while being here in Texas and God allowed us to experience living on each side of town. God connected me with a beautiful sister in Christ who's been following my platform since day one and she introduced me to some realtors that God previously connected her to. She gave me their information, I didn't jump on it right away because I was still fighting doubt, and fear of being denied yet again. but I finally pushed through it and I reached out to them. These realtors were like angels from heaven. They were a beautiful couple who were also believers of Christ and had a passion to help God's children. I told them my story and my testimony, and they jumped right on the search to find me a home. They gave me a list of houses that I looked through and one of them really caught my eye ,so they reached out to the owner of that property, and for some strange reason, the owners were reluctant on proceeding with my application. They couldn't understand my income, sidenote: when walking with God nothing will ever make sense on paper. But they were still very reluctant so my realtors decided to look elsewhere for a place for me. I want you to also keep in mind that I'm doing all of this without regular paystubs, and without working a 9 to 5. All I had was bank statements of my income from the blessings that God used people to pour into me with.

In the meantime, of them looking for places for me, I asked my sister to ask the owner of the Airbnb she was currently residing in if I could rent the empty bedroom. At first, the landlord was OK with it but when she found out I had three kids, she changed her mind and said no she couldn't rent it out to me. During the same time, I was already living in the Airbnb and I was booked up until April 30. After the 30th I knew I had nowhere else to go. My funds were running low and I knew that the money that I saved up was going to be for my new home. Because of that, I was in a rush to find a place so I wouldn't have to keep tapping into my funds that I had saved for my home. April 27, 2024 the realtors Michelle and Michael Prince reached out to me and she said" I found another property for you ,I will send you the house so you can take a look at it and if you like it, I will reach out to the property owner to see if we can get you in". When I received this call, I was on my way to the beach with my kids and my sister in Christ and her children as well but it was such a urgency that I had to pull over to park to look at the property . I then contacted the realtors and told them that I was interested. They immediately contacted the owner of the property and she told them that she wanted to speak with me. I then reached out to the owner and she asked me a few questions, sent over an application, I filled out the application and she mentioned to me that she can get me in the home by May first.

When she said that I knew it was God because after April 30, I had no idea where I was going to go and again, I was running low on funds. So I filled out the application , submitted it over and submitted my prayer to God and asked that God's will shall be done. Monday morning during my devotion time with the Lord, He gave me a specific revelation of good news coming my way through the number 1309 and that means tidings, reward for good news /tidings.

He told me that I will be moving into my home in May. He told me that the home has already been prepared and he sent angels ahead of me to prepare the way (Exodus 23:20).

Shortly after sitting with the Father and receiving this revelation, I received a text message from the property owner saying that I was approved and she requested me to come view the property for the next morning. I couldn't do nothing but shout for joy and dance, and praise God's holy name because I have received denials after denials after denials and I finally got my approval. I told my kids and we all celebrated and packed our belongings. Not only did I know that I would be viewing my home the next day but by faith I knew that I would also be moving into my new home. I know God is a God who performs 11th hour miracles!!

The next day came, which was the last day the Airbnb was booked up to and we got on the road and drove to the property. On the way there to the new property I seen a big truck ahead of us and it had Keith written on the back of the truck. It comforted me because if you don't know, my father passed away July 2022 and his name is Keith. But it gets even better, as I was getting off the exit after driving an hour from the airbnb to go to the new home, the exit was called Wilson Road. Keep in mind my father's name is Keith Wilson. At that point I was blown away because I knew that this was certainly ordained by God. We pulled up to the property and viewed the first house, but for some reason, I wasn't really impressed, it didn't have enough space for me and the kids, but I was still desperate for a home. I heard God say "don't settle".

The property manager mentioned that they had another house that was on the market, but someone else was planning to move into that home and she said if I wanted to take a look at that home, I can. She also mentioned that if I wanted to move into the house that we first viewed, we would be able to move in that very same day but If I had decided on moving into the other listing she would have to reach out to the people who were interested in renting that property, and we would have to wait to see if they wanted to move forward or not. So basically I wouldn't be able to move into the bigger home on that day because I would've had to wait for the other applicants to make their decision. She said she wouldn't know until the end of business day or the until the next day if I will be able to move into the bigger home. By faith, we walked over a few houses down and viewed the other property which was also a bigger property and my children was sold. I fell in love immediately. It was more than enough space for me and my children. I decided to inquire about this property and I trusted and believed that if this was for me, then God will open the door. So, the property manager said I will reach out to the other applicant to see if they want to move forward and I will let you know hopefully today by 4 o'clock . She said worse come to worse I would still be able to move into the first home we viewed. So I decided I would wait around in that area until we find out the verdict. But either way, she was allowing me to move into one of those houses on that day. The kids and i decided to go to the park up the street and park there until I got my answer . About an hour after waiting , I

received my answer. She texted me and said hello Britney we would like to move forward with you on the larger unit. All I need is the security deposit, first month's rent, and proof of renters insurance and I will meet you back at the property at 3:30 with your keys. This whole entire process only took a total of 3 days!! Y'all God really did this thing! Not only that but my street address meant Gabriel, which is the archangel who brings good news. To add to that the property that I was moving into also begin with the letter B and to make mention, this home just finished getting built the month that I moved here to Texas.

This home was specifically built for my family, and I, and as God said to me during my time of devotion, He had already prepared a place for me and that he did. Listen to this, it gets even better. My family on YouTube suggested me to do a virtual housewarming party and I had only set a goal for $3000 but God kept telling me to go higher and I can admit, I disobeyed, and I kept it at $3000. But by the end of that housewarming party, I met my goal and not only was I able to fully furnish my home, but I was also able to pay my rent early in advance for the upcoming month. Only God can do it!!!

There were so many times that I fussed and fought with God because I was tired of being in that situation of being homeless, and I was trying to rush God, instead of trusting Him. In this, I've learned that God's timing is always the best timing, and we have to always trust the process no matter what it looks like. Think about when a caterpillar has to go into a cocoon. The cocoon always looks ugly but when it blossoms into the butterfly from out of the cocoon stage, it ends up looking absolutely beautiful right? Things that God handknits takes time and we have to allow it or else it won't turn out to be the beautiful masterpiece God ordained it to be. God kept taking me to 1st Chronicles chapter 17, and this talks about God's promise to David and how God had promised to build David house. He also said that he will make his name great like the greatest men on earth. As I reflect on this journey, I can honestly say that I'm walking in answered prayers. God has built my house, and He has also used my journey to inspire, empower, and encourage thousands of people. I'm realizing that I am also walking in some of the promises that God has given to David as well and I am so honored, humbled, and blessed to be chosen for such a time as this. God promised me restoration and I am fully walking and living in my season of restoration. I went from living in a two bedroom apartment to being obedient and following Gods instruction of leaving my apartment. Down to living in hotels & Airbnb to us now living in a three bedroom house ,backyard ,2.5 bathrooms ,two car garage ,newly built home in the outskirts of Texas in a safe and quiet neighborhood. You can't tell me that God isn't real!! I know just as God has fulfilled His promise of restoration with my living situation, I am super confident to say that I know it's just a matter of time that the restoration all things including my marriage restoration will come to pass. But right now, I'm living in a season of restoration with relationships and although I had to walk away from my family, I'm so happy and honored to say that God has handpicked these beautiful people that is not only in alignment with the will of God, but also in alignment with my journey who truly has a heart for me, and genuinely celebrates my success.

Made in the USA
Columbia, SC
09 November 2024